Thomas Jefferson and the Empire of Liberty

Torrey Maloof

Consultants

Vanessa Ann Gunther, Ph.D.
Department of History
Chapman University

Nicholas Baker, Ed.D.
Supervisor of Curriculum and Instruction
Colonial School District, DE

Katie Blomquist, Ed.S.
Fairfax County Public Schools

Publishing Credits

Rachelle Cracchiolo, M.S.Ed., *Publisher*
Conni Medina, M.A.Ed., *Managing Editor*
Emily R. Smith, M.A.Ed., *Series Developer*
Diana Kenney, M.A.Ed., NBCT, *Content Director*
Courtney Patterson, *Senior Graphic Designer*
Lynette Ordoñez, *Editor*

Image Credits: Cover and pp. 1, 8 (top), 13, 20 (bottom), 21, 24 Granger, NYC; Cover (image of text) Wikimedia Commons/Public Domain; p. 4 (left) New York Public Library Digital Collections, (center) Thomas Jefferson Papers, Library of Congress, (right) GraphicaArtis/Bridgeman Images; pp. 5, 10 (bottom), 11, 14, 15 (top), 22, 23, 25 (top), 26 (bottom) North Wind Picture Archives; p. 6 Boston Public Library/Internet Archive/Public Domain; p. 7 Jason O. Watson/historical-markers.org/Alamy Stock Photo; p. 8 (middle) New York Public Library Digital Collections, (bottom) Muscarelle Museum of Art; p. 9 (top) The Colonial Williamsburg Foundation, (bottom) Encyclopaedia Britannica/UIG Universal Images Group/Newscom; p. 10 (top) LOC [LC-DIG-csas-05799]; p. 12 LOC [mtjbib000092]; p. 15 (bottom) Papers of Thomas Jefferson, Manuscript Division, Library of Congress; p. 16 Courtesy of the Trustees of the Boston Public Library/Rare Books; p. 18 Courtesy of the Getty Museum; p. 19 Sarin Images/Granger, NYC; p. 20 (top) Perry-Castañeda Library Map Collection, University of Texas at Austin; p. 25 (bottom) Tracy W. McGregor Library of American History, Special Collections, University of Virginia Library; p. 26 (top) Thomas Sully, Portrait of Thomas Jefferson, begun 1821, finished 1830; oil on canva, 37.5 x 32.5 inches; American Philosophical Society. Gift of William Short, 1830; p. 27 (top) KEYSTONE Pictures USA/ZUMAPRESS.com; pp. 27 (bottom), 29 (back) Michaela McNichol/Library of Congress; p. 28 Thomas Jefferson to John Adams, June 10, 1815. Manuscript letter. Manuscript Division; p. 29 (front) ©Thomas Jefferson Foundation at Monticello; p. 31 Courtesy of the Diplomatic Reception Rooms, U.S. Department of State; p. 32 Courtesy of the Trustees of the Boston Public Library/Rare Books; all other images from iStock and/or Shutterstock.

Library of Congress Cataloging-in-Publication Data

Names: Maloof, Torrey, author.
Title: Thomas Jefferson and the Empire of Liberty / Torrey Maloof.
Description: Huntington Beach, CA : Teacher Created Materials, 2017. | Includes index. | Audience: Grade 4-6.
Identifiers: LCCN 2016034135 (print) | LCCN 2016036959 (ebook) | ISBN 9781493837922 (pbk.) | ISBN 9781480757578 (eBook)
Subjects: LCSH: Jefferson, Thomas, 1743-1826--Juvenile literature. | Presidents--United States--Biography--Juvenile literature.
Classification: LCC E332.79 .M35 2017 (print) | LCC E332.79 (ebook) | DDC 973.4/6092 [B] --dc23
LC record available at https://lccn.loc.gov/2016034135

Teacher Created Materials
5301 Oceanus Drive
Huntington Beach, CA 92649-1030
http://www.tcmpub.com

ISBN 978-1-4938-3792-2

Printed by: 51497
Printed in: China

Table of Contents

Exploration and Liberty

In 1780, the United States was in the midst of war. It was fighting for its independence. It had been at war with Great Britain for five years. It was at this time that Thomas Jefferson penned a letter to his friend George Rogers Clark. In the letter, he wrote about the United States. He hoped that one day it would expand westward. It would be more than 13 colonies. It would drive past the Mississippi River. He longed for the United States to be an "empire of liberty."

Jefferson's 1780 letter to Clark

[George Rogers Clark]

George Rogers Clark

Thomas Jefferson

FAMOUS CLARK

George Rogers Clark lived on the frontier. He and Jefferson **corresponded** through letters for many years. Clark's youngest brother was the famous William Clark of the Lewis and Clark expedition!

Americans hold off British troops during the American Revolution.

Jefferson felt that the United States had great potential. It could be a free country founded on the idea that "all men are created equal," an idea he wrote about in the Declaration of Independence. It could grow and expand in the name of liberty. Jefferson dedicated his life to this vision of his country. He served as secretary of state to George Washington. He was vice president to John Adams. And then, in 1800, he was elected the third president of the United States. During his two terms in office, he did as he had always hoped. He pushed the country westward. He took great strides toward creating his "empire of liberty." Thomas Jefferson helped create the United States of America we know today.

Finding His Place

A **plantation** stood at the foothills of the Blue Ridge Mountains in the Virginia colony. This was where Thomas Jefferson was born on April 13, 1743. He was the third of 10 children. Jefferson was all red hair and freckles. He loved the wilderness surrounding the family plantation. He enjoyed exploring nearby trails and valleys with his father. He kept notes in journals about the different plants and animals he saw on his outings. As he got older, he liked to go hunting and fishing with his friends.

The young Jefferson also loved to read. He was a gifted learner. First, he was taught by a tutor. Later, he attended a boarding school where he studied classical languages. When he was older he wrote that "to read Latin and Greek authors in their original, is a sublime luxury."

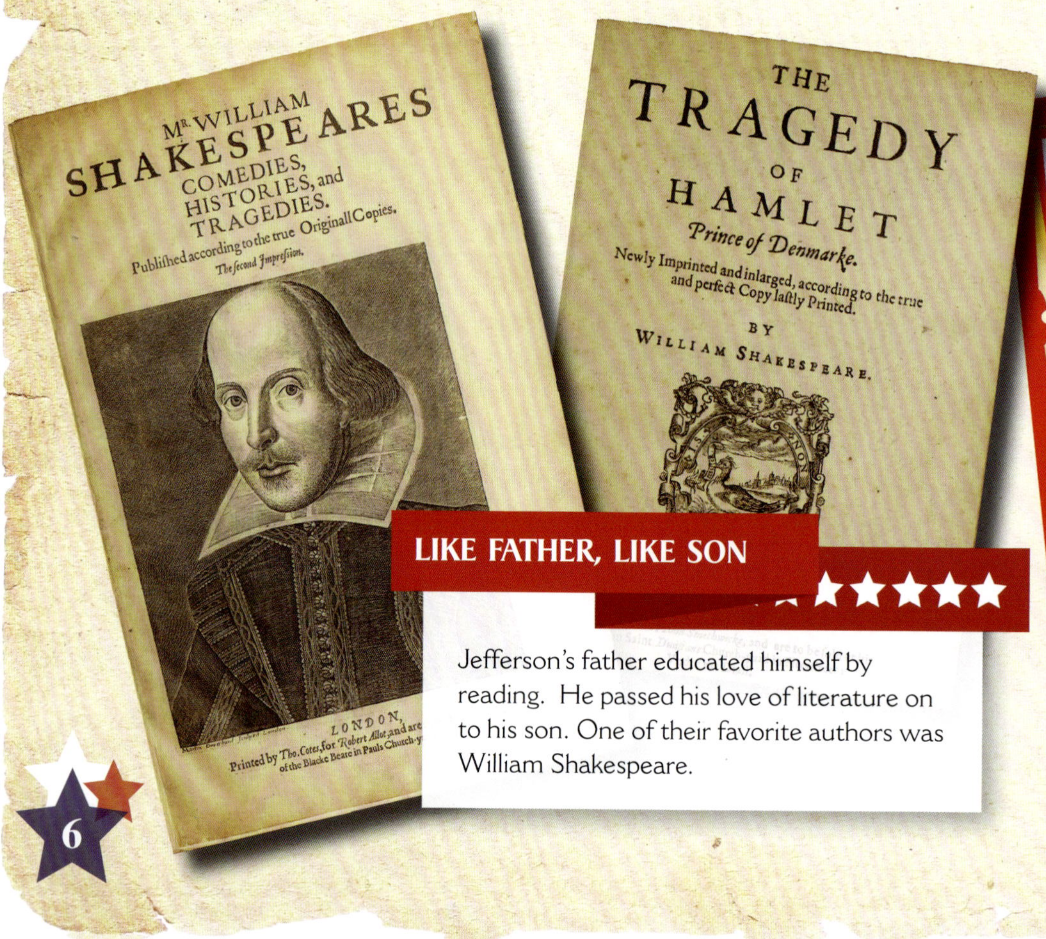

LIKE FATHER, LIKE SON

Jefferson's father educated himself by reading. He passed his love of literature on to his son. One of their favorite authors was William Shakespeare.

After boarding school, Jefferson was taught by **Reverend** James Maury. He taught other students in the area, too. Jefferson spent weekdays learning at the reverend's home. He studied literature, history, philosophy, and science. On the weekends, he returned home. He needed to help his mother run the plantation. His father had died in 1757. This had made the 14-year-old Jefferson the man of the house.

This sign marks the location of Maury's School in Gordonsville, Virginia.

Blue Ridge Mountains in Virginia

In 1760, Jefferson moved to Williamsburg. It was the capital of Virginia at the time. It was there that he attended the College of William & Mary, the second-oldest college in the United States. (Harvard is the oldest.)

Jefferson enjoyed life in the city. He got to do things he had never done before. He went to the theater and attended concerts. There were horse races on Saturdays and dances in **taverns**. But he spent most of his time studying. He graduated from college in just two years.

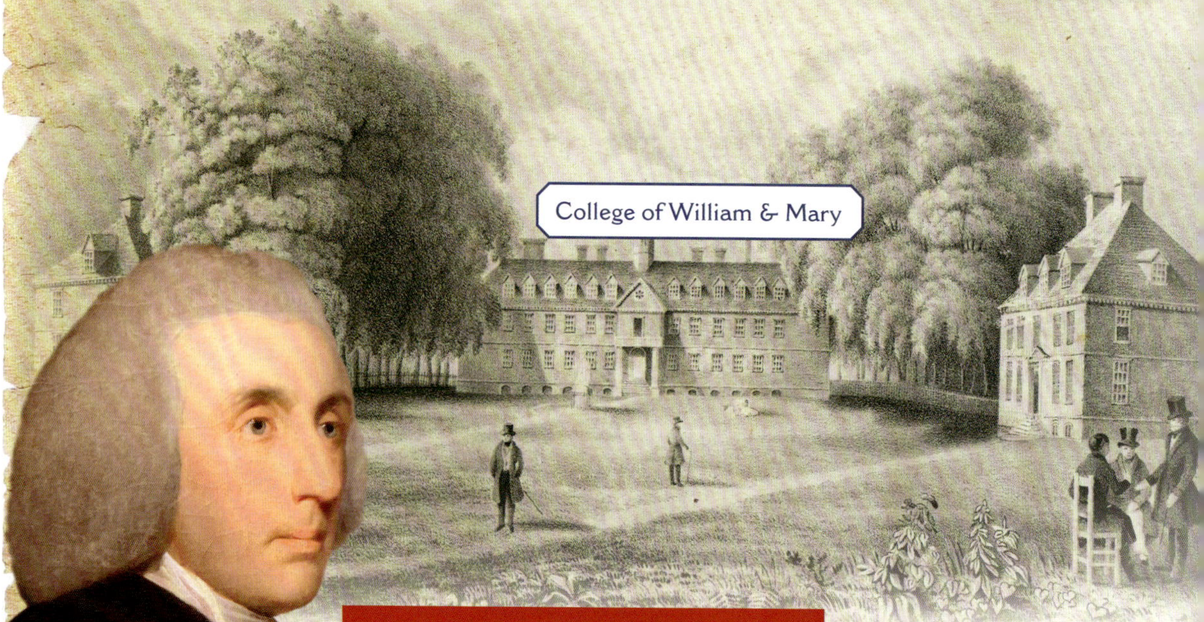

College of William & Mary

Dr. William Small

GOOD INFLUENCES

Jefferson became close friends with Dr. William Small. He was a math professor at the college. Jefferson admired Small's enthusiasm for learning. Small introduced Jefferson to George Wythe.

re-enactment of a trial in colonial Williamsburg

After college, Jefferson decided to study law. There were no law schools in colonial America. Back then, it was customary to learn about law from books and well-established lawyers. Jefferson studied under a lawyer named George Wythe (WITH). He was known for being an honest man and was well liked in the community. Jefferson spent five years learning from Wythe. The two formed a close friendship. Jefferson later referred to Wythe as his "second father."

In 1767, Jefferson started his own law practice. He worked on more than 900 cases during his law career. But the law was not the only thing Jefferson was interested in during this time. He quickly became engrossed in **politics**.

GEORGE WYTHE

George Wythe lived an impressive life. He was a lawyer and a politician. He signed the Declaration of Independence and helped frame the U.S. Constitution. He later became the first law professor in the United States. Jefferson once said about Wythe that "his virtue was of the purest tint; his integrity inflexible, and his justice exact...."

George Wythe

The House of Burgesses met in this room in Williamsburg, Virginia.

Jefferson's daughter, Martha

A GROWING FAMILY

On New Year's Day in 1772, Jefferson married Martha Wayles Skelton. Jefferson and Martha shared a profound love of music and reading. Their marriage was a happy one. The couple had six children together, but only two lived to adulthood.

Jefferson, like many colonists at that time, was not happy with Great Britain. He felt that the king was doing a poor job of ruling the American colonies. Jefferson thought the colonists should be able to make their own laws. So, he looked to a group that he thought could help.

The House of Burgesses was a group of representatives. It was the oldest **legislature** in the United States. They met to discuss and make laws for the Virginia colony. However, Great Britain could veto, or reject, any laws that were made. It was still the reigning authority in the colony. To join the house, men had to be elected. In 1768, Jefferson decided to run for a seat in the house. And he won! This was the first step in his political career.

As time went on, tensions between the colonists and Great Britain grew. Colonists were tired of being taxed without representation in the British government. They were fed up. It was time for a change. Jefferson had **revolutionary** ideas about what the colonies could do, and he was ready to share them.

Colonists protest British taxes.

Writing a Declaration

Jefferson felt that the colonies needed to come together. They would have more power if they were united as one. So, Jefferson helped form the Committees of Correspondence. Each colony chose a group of men to share news and information from their colony with the leaders of the other colonies. This way, everyone was on the same page.

Jefferson was never a confident speaker. His power rested in his pen. In 1774, he wrote an important political **essay**. It was called "A Summary View of the Rights of British America." In it, he asked for the king to be sensible. He believed a king should help his people, not hurt them. He explained that the British government did not have the right to rule the colonies. The people of the colonies had been free and independent from day one. He said that liberty was a human right. It was given to them by nature, not by a king. These ideas were bold and **controversial**. Jefferson was brave to write about them.

The ideas and language Jefferson used in his essay would help him write another important document. This one would change the world.

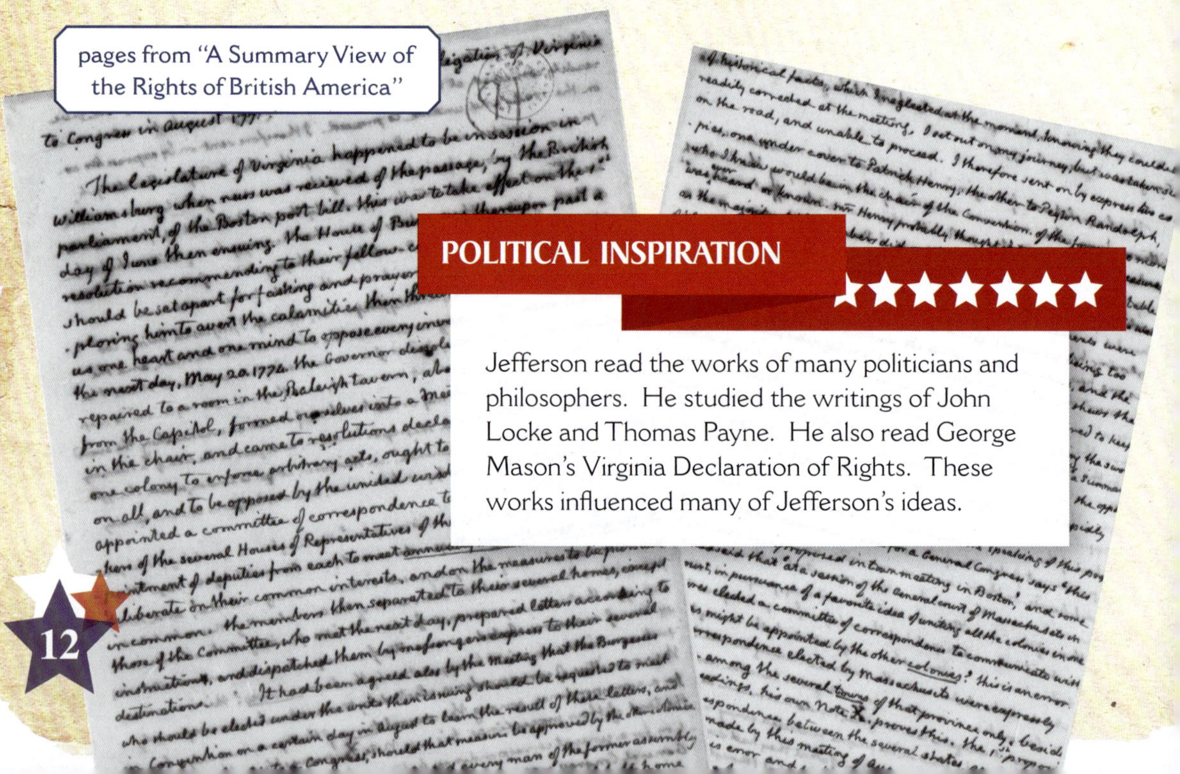

pages from "A Summary View of the Rights of British America"

POLITICAL INSPIRATION

Jefferson read the works of many politicians and philosophers. He studied the writings of John Locke and Thomas Payne. He also read George Mason's Virginia Declaration of Rights. These works influenced many of Jefferson's ideas.

BUILDING MONTICELLO

When Jefferson was a boy, he found a spectacular hillside and dreamed of living there. In 1769, he began building his home there. He named the house Monticello (mon-ti-CHEL-oh). That means "little mountain" in Italian.

Thomas Jefferson forms the Committees of Correspondence in 1773.

Jefferson strongly believed that if a government did not protect the rights of its citizens, then those citizens had a right to **abolish** that government. They had a right to create a new one. The king had ignored the colonists' many requests for change. There were now serious talks about the colonies declaring independence. Jefferson supported this idea.

In April of 1775, shots were fired in Lexington and Concord. Colonists were now fighting the British. The war had begun. The Second **Continental Congress** met many times during the next year. The men debated what they should do. They finally agreed it was time to break free from Great Britain. An official document was needed. It would tell the world the reasons why the United States was now its own nation. But who would write it? The Congress knew the perfect man for the job.

In June of 1776, Jefferson began drafting the Declaration of Independence. It took him only 17 days to write the words that would change the world. A group called the Committee of Five reviewed the draft and made several changes. It was then given to the Congress. It was approved on July 4, 1776. The words Jefferson wrote moved Americans. They inspired people around the world. Those words continue to inspire people today.

Colonists fight the British in the Battle of Lexington.

Thomas Jefferson writes the Declaration of Independence.

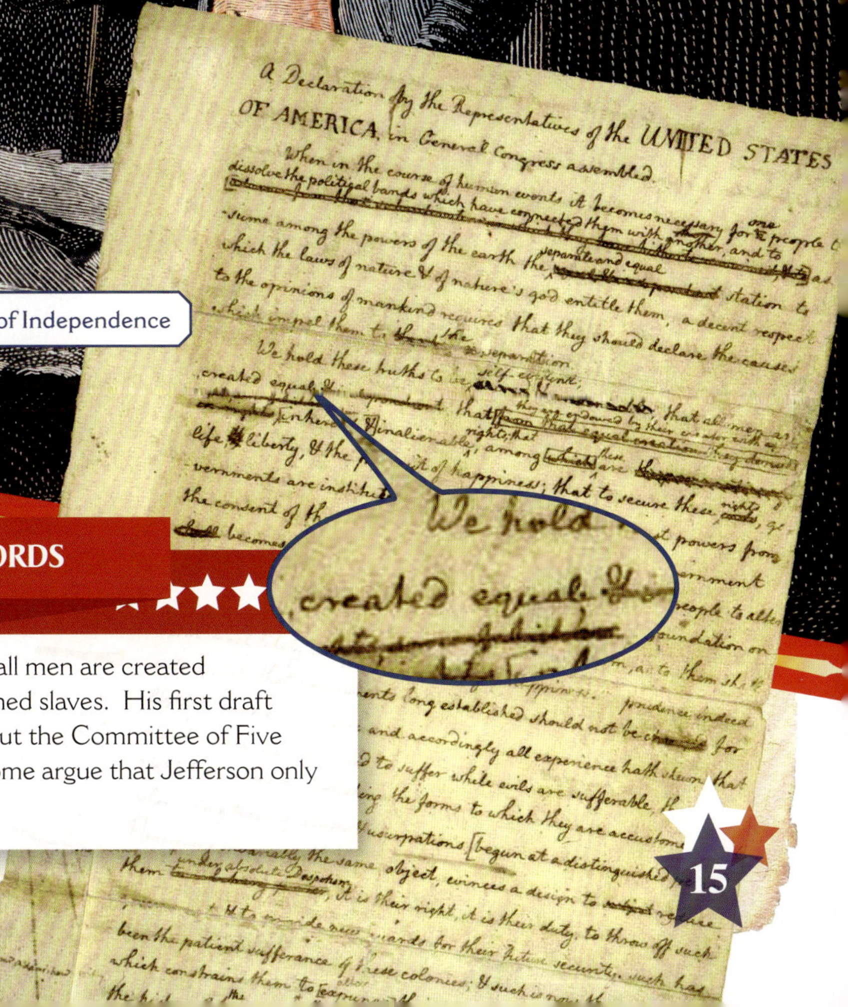

early draft of the Declaration of Independence

CONTROVERSIAL WORDS

Jefferson wrote that "all men are created equal," and yet he owned slaves. His first draft condemned slavery. But the Committee of Five removed that part. Some argue that Jefferson only meant white men.

Serving the New Nation

After signing the Declaration, Jefferson returned home. He missed his family. And he knew he would be needed in Virginia. Now that the country had declared its freedom, the state would need its own set of laws. While the war waged on, Jefferson worked on writing and passing new laws.

Jefferson thought everyone should have the right to an education. He proposed that public schools be built in each county. Sadly, this law was not passed. He also wrote a law about freedom of religion. Jefferson felt that people should have the right to practice the religion of their choice. This was a radical idea at the time. And he wanted a strong separation of church and state. The law stated that churches would not get money from taxes. This law passed in 1786.

In 1779, Jefferson was elected governor. This was a difficult time to be a leader. The state had very little money. And British troops were headed south. Jefferson was discouraged when the enemy invaded his state. He struggled to lead as governor. So, in 1781, he **resigned**.

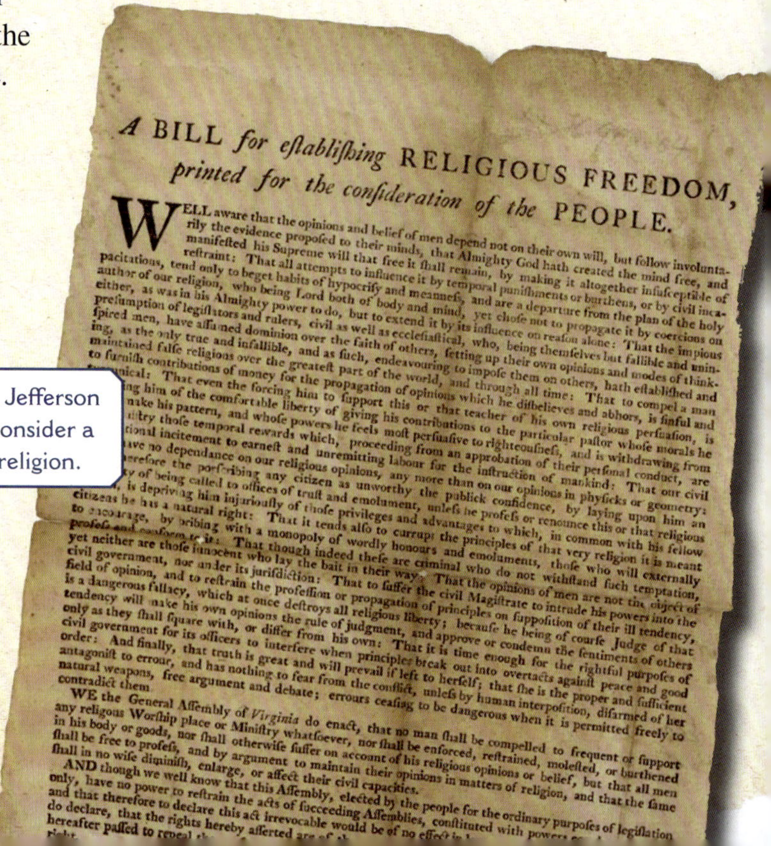

A BILL for *establishing* RELIGIOUS FREEDOM, *printed for the consideration of the* PEOPLE.

This 1779 broadside by Jefferson encourages people to consider a law on the freedom of religion.

NARROW ESCAPE

When the British invaded Virginia, they had orders to capture Jefferson. But Jefferson was warned by a friend. Later, Jefferson saw them coming over a hill through a spyglass. He had escaped just in time.

In 1782, Jefferson suffered a tragic loss. His beloved wife Martha passed away. Jefferson was grief-stricken. He did not leave his room for nearly three weeks. His daughter later wrote that he nearly lost his mind because he was so upset. James Madison was a very close friend of Jefferson's. He suggested that Jefferson return to work. That would keep his mind distracted. In 1783, Jefferson joined the new Confederation Congress. While in office, he helped develop the U.S. **currency**.

In 1784, Jefferson was sent to Paris, France. Congress wanted him to secure friendships with countries in Europe. They wanted him to **negotiate** treaties. Congress hoped Jefferson could persuade other countries to trade with the United States. Jefferson enjoyed his time in France. He was there for five years.

LIKES AND DISLIKES

Jefferson liked French culture. But he greatly disliked the nobility and the monarchy. The government was controlled by the wealthy. It went against everything Jefferson stood for.

Paris in the 18th century

When Jefferson returned home, many things had changed. The United States now had a constitution and a president (George Washington). Jefferson had been appointed to Washington's **cabinet** as secretary of state. It was his job to handle **foreign affairs**. Jefferson often disagreed with his fellow cabinet member Alexander Hamilton on how best to run the country. The two men argued bitterly over many issues. But in doing so, they helped shape the young nation.

In 1796, Jefferson ran for president. But, he lost to John Adams. Because he came in second place based on votes, he was made the vice president. This was the law back then. Jefferson would get another shot at the presidency in four years.

Washington's cabinet (from left to right): Henry Knox, Thomas Jefferson, Edmund Randolph, Alexander Hamilton, and George Washington

Expanding the Nation

In 1800, Jefferson ran for president again. This time, he won! He beat John Adams to become the third president of the United States.

Jefferson had always been fascinated with the vast frontier west of the Mississippi. But France owned this land then. So when an opportunity arose to purchase this land, Jefferson could not refuse.

draft of the speech Jefferson gave when he took office in 1801

map of the Louisiana Purchase

The Louisiana Purchase is signed in 1803.

In 1803, Jefferson sent two of his advisors to France. He wanted to purchase the Port of New Orleans. This port was central to the United States' trade industry. If France sold the port to another nation, the United States would suffer huge **financial** losses. At this time, Napoleon Bonaparte (BOH-nuh-part) was the **emperor** of France. When Jefferson's advisors spoke with Napoleon, they were shocked. He didn't want to sell the Port of New Orleans. Instead, he wanted to sell all the land France controlled in North America! Napoleon needed money for his wars. A deal was quickly made. Jefferson's advisors bought all the land for $15 million! That was about three cents per acre. It was a steal of a deal. The Louisiana Purchase had just doubled the size of the United States. Jefferson was thrilled.

Now, it was time to explore the new land. Jefferson asked his personal secretary, Meriwether Lewis, to lead the journey. Lewis eagerly accepted. Lewis then asked his old friend, William Clark, to be his co-captain.

Lewis promptly began gathering supplies. Congress gave him $2,500 to spend. It was not a lot of money, and the trip cost much more than that. Still, Lewis was able to purchase some of the items he needed. He bought guns and ammunition. He bought tools and food. Medical supplies were purchased, too.

Jefferson asked Lewis to keep a journal. He wanted every detail recorded. He was interested in any scientific discoveries that Lewis might make. What kinds of plants would he see? What kinds of animals would he find? Jefferson was very excited. He could not wait to read all about Lewis's adventures.

There were about 45 men in the group of explorers. Lewis's dog, Seaman, also joined them. In May of 1804, the men set out on their quest. The group faced extreme weather. They tackled bouts of hunger. They dealt with injuries and illnesses. It was a long and dangerous trek. But in November of 1805, they finally reached the Pacific Ocean. It took the group another year to return home. In total, they traveled 8,000 miles (13,000 kilometers)!

pages from Clark's journal

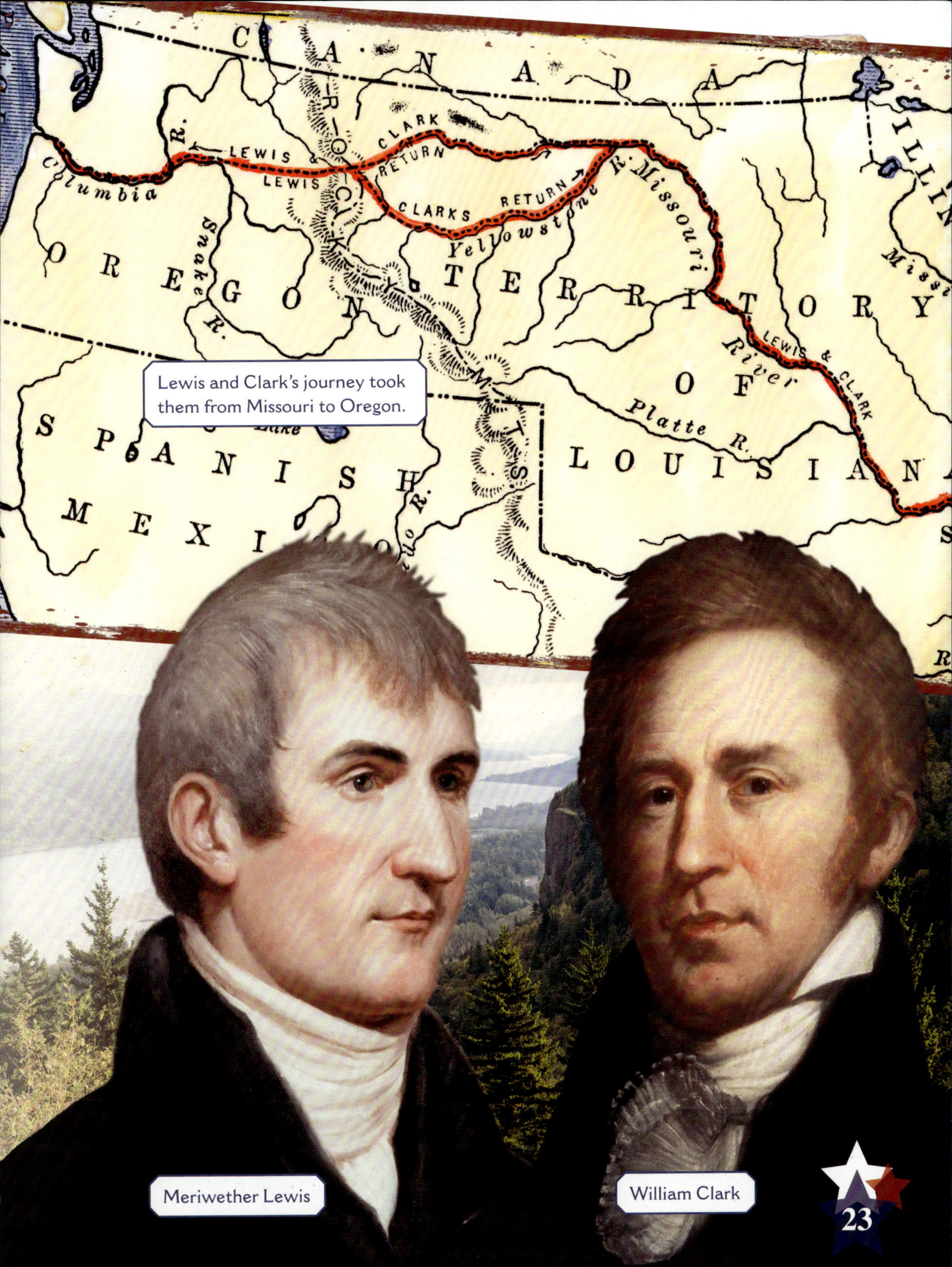

Lewis and Clark's journey took them from Missouri to Oregon.

Meriwether Lewis

William Clark

Toward the end of 1804, Jefferson was reelected for a second term. He was now 61 years old. In this term, his attention was focused on foreign affairs and slavery.

During this time, Great Britain and France were attacking American ships. Jefferson didn't want to engage in a war. But he had to do something. In 1807, the **Embargo** Act was passed. It banned the United States from trading with Europe. Jefferson hoped this would hurt France and Great Britain. He assumed it would force them to negotiate with the United States. But the act failed. The two countries simply traded with other European nations to get the things they needed. This made the United States suffer instead. It had no one else to trade with. The act was **repealed** in 1809.

This 1809 political cartoon shows Jefferson being robbed by France and Great Britain because of the Embargo Act.

enslaved families in the South

During his second term, Jefferson also thought about slavery. He asked Congress to put an end to the slave trade. Jefferson thought that slavery would eventually stop on its own if it was illegal to bring new slaves into the country. In 1807, Congress passed an act that stopped the slave trade, but it did not end slavery. When enslaved people had children, their children also became enslaved. Thus, the slave population grew. And slavery continued for several more decades.

TOO LITTLE TOO LATE

Jefferson owned hundreds of enslaved people. Yet he only freed seven of them. He believed enslaved people should be freed slowly and returned to Africa.

Isaac Granger, an enslaved man at Monticello

Jefferson Dined Alone

In 1809, Jefferson was ready to retire. With his second term over, he returned to Monticello. Even in retirement, Jefferson kept busy. He enjoyed spending time with his grandchildren. And he entertained many guests at his home.

By 1826, Jefferson's health was failing. He spent most of his days in bed. On July 2, he was very weak. He knew his time was coming. But, he was trying hard to hold on. He wanted to live to see July 4. That day would be the 50th anniversary of the approval of the Declaration of Independence. As the United States celebrated the Fourth of July, Thomas Jefferson passed away. He was 83 years old.

Painting of Thomas Jefferson by Thomas Sully

Fourth of July celebration in the early 1800s

President Kennedy (center) with the Nobel Prize winners in 1962

In 1962, President John F. Kennedy hosted a dinner at the White House. It was to honor **Nobel Prize** winners. During his speech, he said that there had never before been a group of such brilliant minds gathered at the White House, except for "when Thomas Jefferson dined alone." This was a clever and fitting tribute to the gifted mind of the man who helped create the United States of America. Jefferson had his flaws. But, he also had his triumphs. He will always be remembered for his thoughts on liberty and his influence on the nation.

BOOK DONATION

During the War of 1812, the British burned the Library of Congress. Jefferson treasured his book collection. But, he sold it to the Library of Congress to replace some of its books. It consisted of 6,487 books!

Sketch It!

Thomas Jefferson loved to read. He once wrote in a letter to John Adams, "I cannot live without books." Today, his life and words fill the pages of dozens of books.

Imagine you could travel back in time to show Thomas Jefferson these books. How do you think he would feel about the way he is remembered? Do you think he would agree with how authors have emphasized different parts of his life? Sketch a comic strip to show how you imagine this conversation.

I have [illegible] met with, and very kindly and opportunely offered me
the means of reprocuring some part of the literary treasures which
I have ceded to Congress to replace the devastations of British Vandal-
ism at Washington. I cannot live without books; but fewer will
suffice where amusement, and not use, is the only future object.
I am about sending him a catalogue to which less than his criti-
cal knolege of books would hardly be adequate. present my high
respects to mrs Adams and accept yourself the assurances of my
affectionate attachment.
Th: Jefferson

Jefferson's letter to John Adams

a recreation of Thomas Jefferson's library at the Library of Congress

This rotating book stand is thought to have been designed by Thomas Jefferson.

Glossary

abolish—to officially end or stop something

cabinet—a small group of people who give advice to the leader of a government

Continental Congress—meeting of colonial leaders to decide how to deal with Great Britain and to decide on laws

controversial—something which is disagreed upon for a long time

corresponded—communicated through letters

currency—a system of money

embargo—a government order that limits trade

emperor—the ruler of a group of regions

essay—a short piece of writing that expresses one's personal views and opinions about a subject

financial—having to do with money

foreign affairs—matters relating to a country outside of one's own

legislature—a group of people who have the authority to make laws

negotiate—formally discuss something in order to make an agreement

Nobel Prize—annual prizes awarded to people in the fields of literature, chemistry, medicine, physics, economics, and peace

plantation—a large farm in the South that produces crops for money

politics—the ways in which governments and leaders do their work

repealed—thrown out, canceled

resigned—formally gave up one's job or position

reverend—a minister or priest in a Christian church

revolutionary—relating to or causing big or important changes

taverns—buildings that provide lodging and food for travelers

Index

Your Turn!

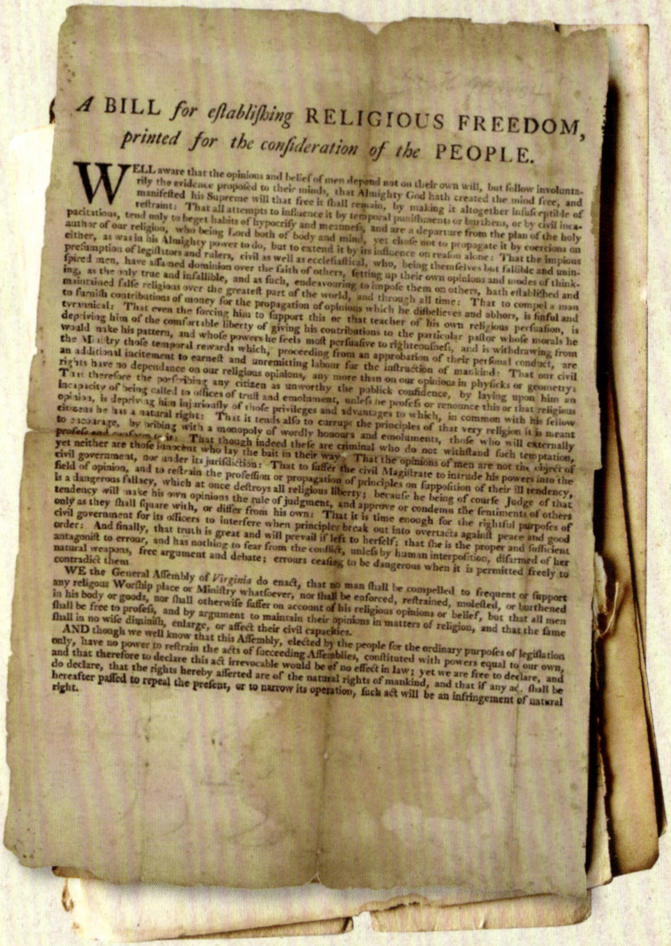

A BILL *for establishing* RELIGIOUS FREEDOM, *printed for the consideration of the* PEOPLE.

WELL aware that the opinions and belief of men depend not on their own will, but follow involuntarily the evidence proposed to their minds, that Almighty God hath created the mind free, and manifested his Supreme will that free it shall remain, by making it altogether insusceptible of restraint: That all attempts to influence it by temporal punishments or burthens, or by civil incapacitations, tend only to beget habits of hypocrisy and meanness, and are a departure from the plan of the holy author of our religion, who being Lord both of body and mind, yet chose not to propagate it by coercions on either, as was in his Almighty power to do, but to extend it by its influence on reason alone: That the impious presumption of legislators and rulers, civil as well as ecclesiastical, who, being themselves but fallible and uninspired men, have assumed dominion over the faith of others, setting up their own opinions and modes of thinking, as the only true and infallible, and as such, endeavouring to impose them on others, hath established and maintained false religions over the greatest part of the world, and through all time: That to compel a man to furnish contributions of money for the propagation of opinions which he disbelieves and abhors, is sinful and tyrannical: That even the forcing him to support this or that teacher of his own religious persuasion, is depriving him of the comfortable liberty of giving his contributions to the particular pastor whose morals he would make his pattern, and whose powers he feels most persuasive to righteousness, and is withdrawing from the Ministry those temporal rewards which, proceeding from an approbation of their personal conduct, are an additional incitement to earnest and unremitting labour for the instruction of mankind: That our civil rights have no dependance on our religious opinions, any more than on our opinions in physicks or geometry: That therefore the proscribing any citizen as unworthy the publick confidence, by laying upon him an incapacity of being called to offices of trust and emolument, unless he profess or renounce this or that religious opinion, is depriving him injuriously of those privileges and advantages to which, in common with his fellow citizens he has a natural right: That it tends also to corrupt the principles of that very religion it is meant to encourage, by bribing with a monopoly of wordly honours and emoluments, those who will externally profess and conform to it: That though indeed these are criminal who do not withstand such temptation, yet neither are those innocent who lay the bait in their way: That the opinions of men are not the object of civil government, nor under its jurisdiction: That to suffer the civil Magistrate to intrude his powers into the field of opinion, and to restrain the profession or propagation of principles on supposition of their ill tendency, is a dangerous fallacy, which at once destroys all religious liberty; because he being of course Judge of that tendency will make his own opinions the rule of judgment, and approve or condemn the sentiments of others only as they shall square with, or differ from his own: That it is time enough for the rightful purposes of civil government for its officers to interfere when principles break out into overt acts against peace and good order: And finally, that truth is great and will prevail if left to herself; that she is the proper and sufficient antagonist to errour, and has nothing to fear from the conflict, unless by human interposition, disarmed of her natural weapons, free argument and debate; errours ceasing to be dangerous when it is permitted freely to contradict them.

WE the General Assembly of *Virginia* do enact, that no man shall be compelled to frequent or support any religous Worship place or Ministry whatsoever, nor shall be enforced, restrained, molested, or burthened in his body or goods, nor shall otherwise suffer on account of his religious opinions or belief, but that all men shall be free to profess, and by argument to maintain their opinions in matters of religion, and that the same shall in no wise diminish, enlarge, or affect their civil capacities.

AND though we well know that this Assembly, elected by the people for the ordinary purposes of legislation only, have no power to restrain the acts of succeeding Assemblies, constituted with powers equal to our own, and that therefore to declare this act irrevocable would be of no effect in law; yet we are free to declare, and do declare, that the rights hereby asserted are of the natural rights of mankind, and that if any act shall be hereafter passed to repeal the present, or to narrow its operation, such act will be an infringement of natural right.

A New Proposition

Thomas Jefferson proposed laws that would allow Americans to receive an education and practice the religion of their choice. This document is the earliest known version of Jefferson's proposal for freedom of religion. What is something that you believe all people should have access to? Write a paragraph stating the problem and how you plan to make changes.